SUPERCONSCIOUS POWER

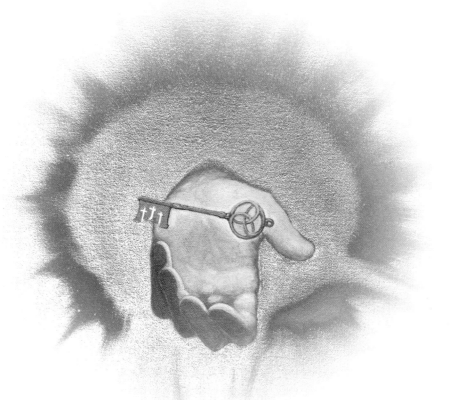

The Science of Attracting Health, Wealth, and Wisdom

MICHAEL MONROE KIEFER Ph.D.

Author: Michael Monroe Kiefer Ph.D.

Title: Superconscious Power

Subtitle: The Science of Attracting Health, Wealth, and Wisdom

Edition: First

Place of Publication: Minnesota, U.S.A.

Published by: Powermind Systems Inc.

Copyright: 2011 Michael Monroe Kiefer Ph.D.

Cover Design: "The Majik Key" by Michael Monroe Kiefer Ph.D. and Guy Smith. The cover design is a trademark owned by Michael Monroe Kiefer Ph.D.

Cover Art: Original oil on canvas painting by Guy Smith.

ISBN 978-0-9645934-4-2

The word "Powermind" is a trademark owned by Michael Monroe Kiefer Ph.D.

Dedicated to my second daughter—
Alexis Monroe Kiefer

"...our brains become magnetized with the dominating thoughts which we hold in our minds..." "These 'magnets' attract to us the forces, the people, the circumstances of life which harmonize with the nature of our dominating thoughts."

Napoleon Hill
Author of, *Law of Success*
Think and Grow Rich
Mental Dynamite

SUPERCONSCIOUS POWER
The Science of Attracting Health, Wealth, and Wisdom

Table of Contents

PROLOGUE

Prophesy of Telepathy! A quote by Dr. Alexander Graham Bell, inventor of the long distance telephone and world-renowned vibrational frequency scientist.

It is important for you to understand that Dr. Bell, a world-renowned vibrational scientist, hypothesized scientifically much of what is in this book back in the early 1900s. Dr. Bell was not considered a quack or a weirdo! He was well respected all over the world for his cutting edge research and inventions. He was considered the top vibrational frequency scientist in the United States! Dr. Bell's invention of the long distance telephone was revolutionary during that time period in American history and he accurately predicted the invention of cell phones decades before technology allowed their creation! You may not grasp the science of what you are about to read in this prologue, but read it anyway! The more you are exposed to mind science, the more you will notice the same exact themes being repeated over and over again in different books. The next time it is presented to you, you will pick up a little more. Eventually, if you are a serious student of superconscious power, you will develop great understanding and true wisdom. This is not gained from reading just one book—however, this book is a good place to start! All mind science revolves around the concepts of energy and vibration, so let's begin!

The human ear can detect vibrations at a rate of 20–40,000 cycles per second (frequency). This is known as sound. As frequency increases higher than 40,000 cycles per second, a human ear cannot hear it anymore—however, one can detect this higher frequency of vibration as radiant energy known as heat or infrared radiation. As the cycles continue to increase higher up on the vibrational scale, humans can see and detect red light—and even higher up the vibrational scale, violet light. Higher yet on the scale, the radiant energy now becomes invisible to the human eye and is known as ultra violet light. Still higher up on the frequency scale, where humans cannot detect the radiant energy at all, are rays like X-Rays and gamma rays, which can have a devastating impact on objects and the human body (DNA in particular).

Even higher up on the vibrational scale could be the realm of thought wave energy or superconscious power!

Dr. Bell's Quote:

"Suppose you have the power to make an iron rod vibrate with any desired frequency in a dark room. At first when vibrating slowly, its movement will be indicated by only one sense, that of touch. As soon as the vibrations increase, a low sound will emanate from it and it will appeal to two senses. At about 32,000 vibrations to the second, the sound will be loud and shrill. But at 40,000 vibrations, it will be silent and movements of the rod will not be perceived by touch. Its movements will be perceived by no ordinary human sense.

From this point up to about 1.5 million vibrations per second, we have no sense that can appreciate any effect of the intervening vibrations. After that stage is reached, movement is indicated first by the sense of temperature, then when the rod becomes red hot, by the sense of sight. At 3 million vibrations, it sheds violet light. Above that, it sheds ultraviolet rays and other invisible radiation—some of which can be perceived by instruments and employed by us.

Now it has occurred to me that there must be a great deal to be learned about the effect of those vibrations in the GREAT GAP where the ordinary human senses are unable to hear, see, or feel the movement. The power to send wireless messages by ether vibrations is in that gap (40,000 to 1.5 million cycles per second). The gap is so great that it seems there must be much more. You must make machines practically to supply new senses as the wireless instruments. Can it be said when you think of that great gap, that there are not many forms of vibrations that may give us results as wonderful as or even more wonderful as the wireless waves?

It seems to me that in this gap may be the vibrations that we have assumed to be given off by our brains and nerve cells when we think. But then again, they may be higher up beyond the scale of vibrations that produce the ultraviolet rays. Do we even need a wire to carry these vibrations? Will they not pass through the ether without a wire just as easily as the wireless waves do? How will they be perceived by the recipient? Will he hear a series of signals or will he find that another man's thoughts have entered his brain?

We may indulge in some speculations based on what we have known of the wireless waves, which I have said are all we can recognize of a vast series of vibrations which theoretically must exist. If the thought waves are similar to the wireless waves, they must pass from the brain and flow endlessly around the world and the universe. The body and the skull and other solid obstacles would form no obstruction to their passage as they pass through the ether which surrounds the molecules of every substance, no matter how solid and dense.

You ask if there would not be constant interference or confusion if there were other peoples' thoughts flowing through our brains and setting up thoughts in them that did not originate with ourselves (inception). How do you know that other men's thoughts are not interfering with yours now? I have noticed many phenomena of mind disturbances that I have never been able to explain. For instance, there is the inspiration or discouragement that a speaker feels in addressing an audience. I have experienced this many times in my life and have never been able to define exactly the physical cause of it.

Many recent scientific discoveries, in my opinion, point to a day not far distant, perhaps, when men will read one another's thoughts—when thoughts will be conveyed directly from brain to brain without intervention of speech, writing, or any of the present known means of communication. It is not unreasonable to look forward to a time when people will see without eyes, hear without ears, and talk without tongues. Briefly, the hypothesis that mind can communicate directly with mind rests on the theory that thought or vital force is a form of electrical disturbance—that it can be taken up by INDUCTION and transmitted to a distance, either through a wire or simply through the all pervading ether, as in the case of wireless telegraph waves.

There are many analogies suggesting that thought is of the nature of an electrical disturbance, a nerve which is of the same substance as brain is an excellent conductor of electrical current. It is reasonable to believe that only a wave motion of a similar character can produce the phenomena of thought and vital force. We may assume that the brain cells act as a battery and that the current produced flows along the nerves, but does it end there? Does it not pass out of the body in waves which flow around the world unperceived by our senses just as the wireless waves passed unperceived until Hertz and others discovered their existence?"

Every mind, both a broadcasting and receiving station, for vibrations of particular thought frequencies!
TELEPATHY!!!

CHAPTER 1

How Your Mind Works—Conscious, Subconscious, Superconscious— The Computer Analogy

Welcome to one of the most well researched books on personal power and mind science you will EVER read! A book meticulously crafted based on personal experiences and research studies of hundreds of adults and teens. A book with the power to "EVOLUTIONIZE" your life! This book will dramatically increase your awareness of why you are, where you are in life—and if needed, show you exactly how to change that...fast!

I am the "chief skeptic" when it comes to cosmic foo-foo, mystic mumbo jumbo, spooky superstitions, and pseudopsychology. I spent much of my early life debunking unscientific psychic phenomenon, false paranormal activity, stage show hacks, money grubbing charlatans, etc. However, solid science supports the truth of what you are about to read. Being formally educated and well trained in the hard science of molecular biology, genetic engineering, psychology, and even more esoteric topics, I have learned it takes blind faith combined with total ignorance to rebuke what is written here. Anyone who has been an astute observer of their life and the lives of those close to them will relish in this book!

The book is carefully crafted to follow a step-by-step sequential pattern, laying out principals and techniques systematically. Stay with each chapter as they build your knowledge base and practice with the techniques as you go to develop your skill. Even if you don't fully understand the science behind the methods, keep reading and stay with it. DON'T QUIT! Concepts will become clearer as you continue to read and practice. I will be your trainer from afar as we embark on our glorious journey together, learning the lessons of how to consciously control the awesome power you possess, known as your superconscious mind! Let's roll!

Your mind is conceptually composed of three distinct entities—conscious, subconscious, and superconscious. Each has specific characteristics and functions. It is important for you to understand the basics of each for the purpose of utilizing this book. I go into much greater depth on the three minds in my first book, *The Powermind System, Power of Will*. However, a snapshot version and a simple analogy will aid most readers in understanding the correct principles for performing the techniques in this book including "superconscious thought induction".

I will now discuss the conscious mind's characteristics and functions. The conscious mind: A) only operates while you are awake or conscious, B) has an important limiting characteristic in that it is only capable of "linear processing" of data, C) can hold only one thought at a time (for our computer analogy, you can view your conscious mind as what is "on screen" on a computer at any given moment), D) operates in conjunction with your subconscious mind, E) acts as an "instructor" or operator and can give instructions to the subconscious mind and finally, F) can alter your subconscious core.

The second entity of mind for our discussion is the subconscious mind. It's main characteristics and functions are as follows.

A) The subconscious mind houses your entire memory bank of experiences since about three months after conception to now. These memories are all the things you have ever experienced, both real and imagined. B) The subconscious mind never sleeps. It operates twenty-four hours a day and is most active during sleep when the conscious mind is turned off. C) It also houses your subconscious core. The subconscious core is your belief system of how you view yourself and interpret the world around you. It is how you measure the reality and truth of information entering your conscious mind. Note: most people have a severely damaged subconscious core, meaning they harbor deep-seated false beliefs about themselves and their environment. For example, an anorexic person may truly believe himself or herself to be overweight in their subconscious core, even though that is a false reality. Another example: a person whom was told by a second grade teacher or parent that they were stupid may still actually harbor that false belief about themselves, although they may now be 30 years old and hold a Master's degree. Core damage is a major limiting factor in most people's lives and I will discuss it in great depth in later chapters.

D) The subconscious mind also operates as a "network processor" of data, much like the internet search engines. It can instantly network and access all of the information in its memory bank. This is a very important fact! E) It also accepts instructions, commands, emotionalized thoughts and affirmations given to it from the conscious mind, both real and imagined!

Let's prove the network processing and command function interaction of the conscious mind and subconscious mind with an example. This is a very important concept for you to grasp early on. For example, let's say I ask you to recall the earliest birthday you can remember. Your conscious mind instructs your subconscious to do a memory search, and it "pops" the earliest memory up to your conscious mind. The subconscious searches all of your memories super fast and acts as a "network processor". If your subconscious mind acted as a linear processor (like your conscious mind does), and only had moment-to-moment or thought-to-thought processing capability, you would do a "linear search" process such as this: *What happened yesterday, and the day before, and the day before, etc?* You would do this "linear search" each day from today and go back until you reached your earliest birthday you could remember. That process of searching would take weeks! Of course, no one's mind works like that!

As we have learned in this first chapter, the conscious mind uses the subconscious mind continuously to assimilate, process, and feedback information. It uses the subconscious core as a frame of reference to measure your truth and reality. The conscious mind can instruct and command the subconscious mind on a surface level to recall information and on a deep "core belief" level.

The conscious mind is a linear thought-to-thought processor, while the subconscious mind is a high-speed network processor that can instantly access all of your experiences, real or imagined. The subconscious mind is the seat of your memory bank and "core belief" system—for our computer analogy, the conscious mind is what is on screen, and the subconscious is like a hard drive and expanded memory.

Lastly, the third entity of mind is the superconscious mind. It is your spirit or soul. It is the essence of why this book was written. I understand many readers will now have some subconscious "core belief" system difficulty here. This is simply because of incorrect childhood conditioning. I was the biggest non-believer for many years. I did not believe in any sort of God, Spirit, or "soul stuff". Science was my God and everything could all be recreated in a test tube or a research laboratory—or so I thought? But after diligently researching for 30+ years now, learning from my own personal experiences and from those of my students, I now have an excellent working knowledge of the superconcious mind. There actually is no conflict with hard physical science and what is in this book. You just have to know where to look to find the hard scientific research. Modern western science hides this information from the general public and belittles the facts as weird mysticism or foolish magic tricks. At any rate, it is not my purpose to argue the point of what I already know. I did that decades ago, and wish to share the real scientific research with you through this book.

The superconscious mind has access to all of humankind's knowledge—which some call the Akashic records. It is the seat of ESP and supernatural power, and operates in conjunction with the subconscious core. Just as the conscious mind operates as commander and instructs the subconscious, the subconscious core commands and instructs or INDUCES the superconscious mind to action. Deeply held beliefs in one's subconscious core induce the superconscious mind to action.

Back to our computer analogy. Imagine if the internet held all of humankind's knowledge—from the beginning of time to the end of time—like God, all knowing, Akashic records, etc. The superconscious or spiritual component of mind could access this information. But, since the superconscious mind is indeed spiritual, it can also provide SOME superhuman, supernatural power.

Through subconscious core belief programming or reprogramming, the superconscious mind is induced to action (superconscious thought induction)!

In conclusion, we have a conscious, subconscious, and superconscious mind uniting and operating as one. The conscious mind instructs the subconscious, the subconscious core induces the superconscious, the superconscious can access all knowledge and can also operate in a supernatural fashion.

However, the flow of information and power is not one-way—the subconscious feeds back important information to the conscious mind and the superconscious can influence both the subconscious and conscious minds. However, the superconscious mind can do MUCH, MUCH more as you will see later in this book! The superconscious mind can operate outside of the known physical boundaries of the human body, dramatically impacting the world around you!

CHAPTER 2

The Principle of Perfect Mental Alignment—The Concept of Mental Radio

Your first objective, in order to induce superconscious power, is to gain perfect mental alignment between your conscious, subconscious, and superconscious minds. Easier said than done! One way to do this is to decisively focus on a very clear, specific goal, or small set of 3–4 goals. This goal must pervade your conscious mind and be driven deep into your subconscious core. It can be a health goal, an income goal, a relationship goal, an education goal, even a hobby goal. The goal must be consciously focused and concentrated on at least 3 times per day! If you are having difficulty determining your goal or small set of goals, read my first book, *The Powermind System, Power of Will.* I go into great depth on goal setting in that book.

You should begin your day by first focusing on your goal, while you are still in bed. This is the start time to begin thinking about your goal for the day. The second time is sometime after lunch, the third and most important time is just before falling asleep at night. It is also beneficial to incorporate your goal/vision training sporadically throughout the day! The goal must be a consistent thought while you are awake, always present in the back of your mind. You can think about your goal in the form of a self-talk statement, such as an affirmation or as a visual image. Try to vividly see yourself as already having achieved your goal. Imagine how it FEELS emotionally to achieve your goal!

By taking conscious control of your mind, your future, and your goals in this way, you begin to instruct or reprogram your subconscious core. As your subconscious core incorporates this new programming or instruction, it will subsequently induce your superconscious mind to action.

Here is the mental radio analogy. Superconscious thought induction, in one sense, can be perceived as a mental radio. You realize radio station waves of many different frequencies are ever present in the air, all around you. However, you do not see or hear or feel the radio station broadcast waves and would never even know they existed—unless, of course, you had a radio! If you did have a radio, you could simply turn it on and "tune" the radio to the specific frequency or station you wanted to listen to. The radio can be easily "tuned" to receive the specific vibrational frequency of radio waves for any given station and "transforms" that vibrational radio wave signal into voices and music that you can now hear. You can "tune" that radio to a wide variety of frequencies or stations.

As your superconscious mind becomes tuned or activated by your subconscious core, it can now tune into and receive information that you were previously unaware of or even knew existed. It was present all around you, all the time—you just didn't notice it, because you were not tuned in! The type of information that you can now receive with your mind or be made aware of is directly related to your goals. If you consider your thoughts as being vibrational in nature (which they are!), then you will understand the power of your thoughts, and how we can both "broadcast" and "receive" much more information than you ever imagined possible!

You essentially can tune your superconscious mind (mental radio) to receive specific frequencies of information and ideas. However, your superconscious mind also radiates energy and influences people, places, and events that are directly related to your goal and actually starts attracting your goal toward you! The superconscious mind will act as an electromagnet by attracting exactly what you need to successfully see your goal manifested in your life. It converts dreams into reality, thoughts into things. This process is governed by universal law, which I will explain in detail later in this book. However this electromagnetic attraction must happen—it is the law!

The principles in this chapter are very important for you to understand, because this is, in fact, how we actively create our lives. We can do this consciously and have more joy, peace, health, wealth, wisdom, creativity, and lust for living in the process, or we can let outside influences control our daily thoughts, thus shaping our subconscious core. This inevitably results in drifting into an agonizing whirlpool of depression, negativity, lethargy, confusion, self-pity, dependence, poverty, sickness, anger, and ignorance.

The superconscious mind is only induced to a high level of activity if there is clarity and perfect mental alignment between the conscious mind's instructions and the beliefs held in the subconscious core.

CHAPTER 3

Barriers to Perfect Mental Alignment—Viewing Your Past as a Prison or a School— What's Holding You Back?

How you view your past is critical to achieving perfect mental alignment. Your conscious mind goes through thousands of fleeting "surface" thoughts every day. It also goes through many records of stored thoughts in your subconscious memory that are highly emotionally charged, but may be totally false!

The impact of any particular thought on your subconscious core depends on its "emotional charging". All thoughts throughout the day are not equal in subconscious core impact! For example, let's say you have the thought early in the morning that you would really like to have pizza for dinner. This may be a fleeting thought throughout the day and really has little impact on your subconscious core. Let's say, later that same day, your manager at work disciplines you for something that was not your fault. This thought will have a much greater impact on your subconscious core because it is highly emotionally charged, IF it is allowed to enter your core. These two thoughts obviously have different levels of impact on your core and it depends on the amount of "emotional charging" they carry.

Many people are stuck in life because they are viewing their past very negatively and this negative set of emotions are deeply ingrained into their subconscious core. They hold deep-seated sadness, anger, guilt, jealousy, and resentment towards some of the people in their past, like parents, ex-spouse, teachers, or relatives—OR they may be generally angry at their past circumstances or their current circumstances. Deep inside their subconscious core they feel "mad", somehow "cheated" by life, and that the world now "owes them" something because of this "unfair treatment". This is considered severe core damage. This deep-seated subconscious core negativity acts as a psychological prison shackling the person's ability to positively activate their superconscious mind. Consciously they want good things for themselves and to be happy, but subconsciously they have a hardened negative subconscious core. Perfect mental alignment is much easier to read about than to actually do. People tend to hang onto these past hurts and lock them deep inside their core. These are very difficult to expose and hard to heal. These are the principle barriers to perfect mental alignment and activating your superconscious power.

I will give you an illustration. I worked with a young woman for a couple of months years ago. I actually met her mother at one of my accelerated learning seminars and she wanted me to counsel her teenage daughter. Her daughter was having a very hard time passing a college entrance exam. Her mother told me her daughter had always "struggled" in school.

I met the 18-year-old woman at a coffee shop and quickly ascertained her subconscious core barrier. She told me that in second grade her reading teacher told her that she was "mentally retarded" because she read her books using her finger as a guide for her eyes. Many of her classmates made fun of her and teased her during that same time in her life. Her teacher actually wrote a note and told her parents that there was something "wrong" with their daughter and she was "learning-disabled". This false information was incorporated into this teenager's subconscious core belief system.

I told this woman that she was in fact a natural speed reader and could assimilate information 2–3 times faster than the average person and probably had other untapped gifts. I showed her a booklet I wrote and use in one of my seminars where I teach people how to double and triple their reading speed using the very same technique she naturally used. She was absolutely stunned! I coached her on improving her reading speed even further over the next few weeks. I also taught her advanced skills in memorization, note taking, exam preparation, and test taking. She picked all of it up fast! A quick study she was. This young lady was harboring a deep-seated false belief about herself and it was locked tight inside her subconscious core for over 10 years! It was about to stop her from attending college! Needless to say, she did quite well on the entrance exam (after having failed it twice before!) and was admitted into the college of her choice. Her mother was totally amazed at her daughter's change in attitude, new level of self-esteem, self-confidence, and positive outlook on life!

Here is a personal example. When I was 13 years old my parents got divorced. This had a negative effect on my subconscious core. My mother, sister, and I became outcasts in the small upstate New York town we lived in. My parents had to file for bankruptcy. We lost our home in the process and were kicked out of our church. The town knew our circumstances. To a young teenager, back in the day, this had a severe emotional impact on me and it took a long time to heal my subconscious core. Now, when I visit with some of my daughter's friends' parents at school, I learn that MANY of the parents have been divorced, some two or three times! Now, divorce is commonplace, accepted, no big deal—almost like trading in a car every few years and getting a new one. I find it fascinating, because my childhood experience was nothing like that!

Your past must be reconciled and viewed as a school, something to learn from, NOT a prison that shackles your progress. Your past is the hand you were dealt and you cannot escape nor change it. You will never achieve perfect mental alignment with your conscious, subconscious, and superconscious minds without a clear subconscious core.

CHAPTER 4

Clearing "Chatter" Out of Your Subconscious Core— Modern Day Regression Therapy—Personal Power!

The term "chatter" refers to getting your subconscious mind bogged down, pessimistic and depressed with negative thinking. Severe core damage, as discussed in the previous chapter, is the result, as well as chronic illness (in many cases). Chatter refers to surface thoughts or small, negative, everyday problems such as news, economy, weather, politics, etc. It can mean internalized negative problems from other people too, like friends, relatives, coworkers, etc. Chatter could also be deep seated subconscious core damage such as child abuse. It could also be from post traumatic stress syndrome. You must learn to control this, clear it and especially reject it and shield yourself of it from other people and your environment. It ALL inhibits perfect positive mental alignment. You can still listen to and help your friends and family members, you can still listen to the news, but don't internalize this negative chatter into your subconscious core!

The most common examples of surface chatter are being emotionally involved with sports teams, politics, weather, taxes, clothing, hair styles, trends, video games, social networking, coworkers, the internet, etc. The list goes on and on. I personally know people who get physically ill and depressed when their favorite sports team loses a game, even missing a day of work because of the severe damage to their core and health. I also know people who spend many hours a day playing video games because they are so obsessed on how to get to the next level in the game.

Some people are also totally involved in their friends' relationships, marriages, and how they are raising their children—all negative, useless, energy-draining chatter! I even know a woman who has stewed on getting a divorce for 5 years. She is all locked up on this topic. She thinks about it daily—it is the main thought she holds in her conscious mind. Her whole life will sadly pass her by as she remains paralyzed by her own negative thought patterns and inability to take action. She lives each day in her self-created Alcatraz.

There are more severe forms of chatter including child abuse, neglect, negative relatives, and friends influencing your subconscious core with past or present put downs. Negative emotional chatter can come from someone close to you, like a spouse, or a person we see as having power over us or commanding our respect. These people can be teachers, doctors, clergy, parents, politicians, older siblings, etc. These people are sometimes close to us or we look up to them in some way. This causes the chatter and core damage brought on by negative situations with these people to be far more emotionally charged and damaging than a complete stranger telling you something.

All of this negative chatter must be cleared and constantly monitored in order for the subconscious core to positively activate the superconscious mind.

I am from the modern day school of regression therapy. This means the person must be brought back to the negative past event, revisit it, but NOT relive it! They must revisit it in the light of current circumstances, with a neutral party observer. The experiences must be reasoned out by the person and they need to come to grips with this past negative chatter and heal it. I have taken many people on regression sessions, and it is always liberating for that person when they accept, release, and heal their subconscious core. They come to the realization that their own negative thoughts about their past experiences are what continually cause them lack of progress and many times chronic physical illness too. They then begin to understand they have the personal power to change those thoughts. The experiences can't be taken away, or erased, or buried, but the negative thoughts can be replaced! This is personal freedom and power and the beginning of perfect mental alignment.

Surface chatter is another matter. It is always an ongoing battle since the environment we live in is incessantly bombarded with negativity and false propaganda. Most outside inputs are extremely negative and deceptive in our society—news, TV, video games, politics, many song lyrics. We must always be "on guard", aware, and consciously shielding it out before it has a chance to influence our subconscious core in a negative manner.

Chatter must be replaced with consciously controlled positive thoughts regarding our goals and the good things that are going to happen in our lives. This directly affects our relationships with our families, co-workers, and our environment. We must affirm positively and confidently our self-reliance, independence, self-set goals, good health, self-earned fortunes, and healthy family relationships. We must never be pushed into the negative media onslaught of propaganda, disinformation, deception, racism, false crisis, class warfare, government dependence, poverty, communism, helplessness, confusion, ignorance and illusion...known as society!

A brief on the science of New Thought is in order here. New Thought science is the concept that "Infinite Intelligence", "Spirit", or "God" is ever present all around us. New Thought science holds that conscious thought is a real force and power for good and that most sickness and disease originates in the mind.

It affirms that Divinity dwells within each and every one of us because we are spiritual beings by nature created in the image of our creator. Our mental states, both conscious and subconscious carry forward in our lives and directly affect our future reality.

New Thought science started in the early nineteenth century and embraces all major religious beliefs in that each person has a spiritual component or soul and by free will to choose can use this supernatural soul power to control the law of attraction through disciplined conscious thinking, such as affirmation and visualization or prayer. The law of attraction applies to all atheists as well. So, your particular religious philosophy is irrelevant in regard to utilizing the law of attraction. It is just historically noteworthy that all major religions embrace the same belief in regard to this particular law. It is also historically noteworthy that all physicists and evolutionists that set out to disprove the existence of Infinite Intelligence (God), after analyzing their own data, convert away from atheism! To learn more about the history of New Thought science, study the works of William Walker Atkinson and Dr. Frank Channing Haddock.

CHAPTER 5

Subconscious Core Clearing For Perfect Health— Clinical Research Studies in Psychoneuroimmunology (PNI)

There is a field of medicine called psychoneuroimmunology and it deals, basically, with the effects of the mind and mood on the body. We all realize that our thoughts have physical effects on our bodies—this is a fact. This field measures the endocrine system (hormone levels) in response to mood and stress, among other things. It also measures elements in the blood involved with our immune system in response to what we are thinking in our minds. There exists direct scientific physiological evidence that our minds directly affect hormone, digestive, immune response, blood element levels, heart rate, and blood pressure.

A person under very high stress, mentally filled with negative emotionalized thoughts driven deep into their subconscious core, feels and is sick. The subconscious core affects the body in multiple negative ways, such as high blood pressure, digestive problems, colon problems, a depressed immune system, and imbalanced hormone levels. The same is true with depression. A mind filled with negative depressing thoughts harms the core and physical body dramatically.

Did you ever notice when you are under high stress or depressed, you tend to get sick with a cold or digestive problem or another chronic ailment starts acting up? How about when you are feeling great, happy, driven? You rarely get sick! Your mind and what is in it has both immediate and long-term health effects on your physical body.

When you are shocked or surprised you feel the "rush" of the hormone adrenaline immediately. It does not take a few minutes! Mind/body effects, both positive and negative are immediate!

If a person harbors negative thoughts deep in their subconscious core, these eat away at the body's physical health. Chronic diseases and nagging ailments are the usual result.

One may put up the false argument that some diseases are "genetic" or "inherited" and there is nothing a person can do about that. With all of my formal education in cell and molecular biology, genetics, and genetic engineering,

I can assure you that no genetic disease is "inherited" only the "tendency" to develop the disease is inherited. Even though you may have the "bad genes" there are other factors that determine whether you actually develop the disease or not—your mind and thoughts being one of them!

The keys to good health are many fold. However, having a subconscious core that is "cleared" of all negative thoughts is vital to perfect health. Second, you must on a conscious level not dwell on negative thoughts or emotionalize them into your subconscious core. The third factor is mental alignment.

The only way to rid your conscious mind of negative thoughts is by constant consistent monitoring and thought substitution. Once you find yourself thinking negatively, you must immediately replace that thought with a positive, happy, or goal-oriented thought and dwell on that.

As you clear your subconscious core and consciously monitor your thoughts daily, replacing your negative thoughts with positive ones, you will feel much better and actually be physically healthier!

There is a well-known anomaly in the medical field known as the "placebo effect". In the placebo effect, some patients are NOT given an experimental drug or treatment but they actually get better just as well as or even more than those given the new drug or treatment. They are not told they are given a placebo—they believe the placebo is the real drug. It is their mind and thoughts that are healing their body.

No medical doctor will argue the fact that some people get astounding results even though they receive nothing but the "belief" they are getting a new treatment—a placebo. There is no other explanation for the placebo effect than the one I just gave! Your mind has a tremendous impact on your physical health, period!

Health References

David B. Beaton – Rochester Institute of Technology, Effects of Psychological Disorders on the Immune System

Andrew P. Otchinsky – Rochester Institute of Technology, The Role of Stress on Physiological Disorders

Jason J. Zodda – Rochester Institute of Technology, The Immune System

David B. Beaton – Rochester Institute of Technology, Just Scratching the Surface of Psychoneuroendocrinology

B. Bower – Severe Depression Depresses Immunity, Science News 127, 100.

B. Bower – Questions of Mind Over Immunity, Science News 139, 216–218.

Glazer R. Kiecolt, Glazer, J. K. and Andersen, B. L. – A Biobehavioral Model of Cancer, Stress, and Disease Course, American Psychologist 49, 389–404.

From Acts 5, 12–16 NIV

"The apostles performed many miraculous signs and wonders among the people. And all BELIEVERS used to meet together in Solomon's Colonnade. No one else dared join them, even though they were highly regarded by the people. Nevertheless, more and more men and women BELIEVED in the Lord and were added to their number. As a result, people brought the sick into the streets and laid them on beds and mats so that at least Peter's shadow might fall on some of them as he passed by. Crowds gathered also from the towns around Jerusalem, bringing their sick and those tormented by evil spirits, and ALL of them were healed."

CHAPTER 6

Gaining and Maintaining Fire and Purpose with Life Coaching— A Street Smart Pusher

In one of my re-careering workshops I coined the term "Street Smart Pusher". This term refers to someone who is street smart, experienced, and can give you a push to achieve more than you ever thought you were capable of.

In speaking to hundreds of dislocated workers each year, I have found many of them are highly skilled and well educated, thus making them easily employable. They just need someone to push them mentally to get them going. They tend to get all wrapped up in negativity and have a daily pity party for themselves looking to the Federal government or someone else to solve THEIR problems.

I have also found that greater than 75% of the employed population in the United States have no real life goals at all. This is staggering! They flounder from day to day, careening from wall to wall, simply existing like a starfish or an amoeba or mold. They aren't particularly sad, but they aren't very happy or excited either. They just exist. They get up each day, unsure as to what their true purpose is. They have jobs, food, clothing, shelter, but have a deep, uneasy sense that something is very wrong, that they are spinning their wheels, wasting their lives away. The weekly happy hours, sporting events, concerts, movies, pointless TV shows, violent video games, recreational or prescription drugs and inane hobbies usually takes the edge off, allowing them to briefly escape their purposeless lot in life.

These people definitely need some challenging goals with real meaning to light their fire and get them jazzed up about living and discovering their natural talents! I have assisted many people to go from a life of utter boredom to fire and purpose by laying out a clear set of personal goals and determining their natural talents with a very unusual test!

I have also seen the flames flicker out when people lose a life coach or street smart pusher that could have helped them attain greatness. They drift back so quickly into the cesspool of mass humans living lives with no point. DRONES! The negative daily chatter drowns out their life fire, suffocates their drive.

A life coach can be an invaluable aid in helping a person maintain clarity, keep the daily chatter at bay, and give a steady push to take the necessary action to achieve their self-set goals.

If you are waiting for the Federal government, boss, co-workers, relatives, employer or someone else to set your goals for you, keep this fact in mind: they really don't care about you! In general, this is human nature. Nobody cares more about YOU than YOU do, so take charge of your own mind and life. Set a goal for yourself and work with what I am teaching you here. You will soon come to know self-confidence, self-knowledge, and self-power you never thought humanly possible. Wisdom is knowledge APPLIED!

CHAPTER 7

The Law of Attraction—Getting Whatever You Want—An Introduction to Vibrational Frequency Science

The "law of attraction" is also known as the "great law of Karma", and is written in the Bible as the "law of sowing and reaping", the "universal law of cause and effect", and even in a fifth way as "the law of vibration".

Simply stated, "as you sow (in your mind) so shall you reap (in your environment)". Whatever thoughts we drive into our subconscious core, we also radiate out into the world and similar things are attracted back to us. Like attracts like. This is the law!

If you want happiness, wealth, peace, perfect health, goal achievement, love, etc., you must begin by consciously sowing those thoughts first into your subconscious core. You must drive out the past and present onslaught of negativity as stated in previous chapters!

You are right now attracting the things, events, people, ideas, and plans that harmonize with your subconscious core. If you do not like the things you are attracting and have in your life, simply change your thinking and focus on what you do want to attract! Our thoughts actually produce and emit a certain frequency of energy and, in turn, attract the like frequency of energy back. Negative vibrations attract negative experiences, just as positive vibrations attract positive experiences into our lives. This is the law! The choice is always yours, every moment of every day. You have free will to choose! But you can be much more specific than just focusing on positive experiences. You can actually attract the EXACT things and circumstances you deeply desire.

The law of vibration is crucial to understanding the nature of whom and what we are. Everything in the universe is moving and vibrating at ultra high speeds. Everything is connected—it impacts and has an effect on everything, and everyone else. This is fact! Your body is made up of atoms, all of which are vibrating!

These five interconnected laws mentioned earlier in this chapter sum up the physical and scientific basis for this book. For example, if we drop a small pebble into a still pond, you will see a ripple effect of waves that radiate outward across the entire pond. You will notice that they are strongest at the point of impact! If we drop a big rock into the pond, it creates the same ripple effect. However, the frequency of the waves are different from the ones the pebble produced because the large rock produces more amplitude or power. If we drop a large boulder into the pond, you will see a huge radiating wave effect of yet a different frequency and great amplitude.

This "waves in a pond" example is a good analogy to the superconscious mind. The more clearly focused and mentally driven you are, the more your superconscious mind is induced to radiate and generate energy waves of a specific frequency and amplitude.

The specific thoughts harbored in your subconscious core determines the frequency. The greater your emotional charge, desire, and concentrated conscious effort and alignment, the greater the amplitude or impact of the radiating wave effect. A small desire generates a pebble effect, a great desire, the boulder effect!

Someone with a totally mean, angry, negative subconscious core is like a huge negative boulder dropped into the pond, upsetting the entire pond. Someone with no goals, no focus, and no alignment is like dropping a grain of sand into the Atlantic Ocean. They have miniscule effect or impact. A person with a perfectly aligned mind and positively charged subconscious core is like a meteor hitting the ocean at near light speed creating a gigantic positive tsunami effect! They affect and influence everything and everyone their energy comes into contact with in huge positive waves. An average person would be bowled over in a positive way by their sheer force or "power of will". Their superconscious radiates at such a high amplitude, their impact is astounding!

The Founding Fathers of the United States aligned within themselves and with each other and had this great positive effect to create the United States of America.

An example of a totally negative subconscious core and superconscious would be Adolf Hitler. He was "rotten to the core".

John Hancock, the American revolutionary, so bold in his core conviction, signed his name three times larger than anyone else did on the Declaration of Independence! An important note that escapes American history books is that all of the signers of the Declaration of Independence knew they were signing their death warrant in the off chance that the American revolution failed. They all knew they would be hunted down and executed if they failed, yet Hancock was totally emboldened! He had an iron will.

CHAPTER 8

The Reason for Your Current Situation in Life—Look in the Mirror!

We just learned in the previous chapter that "like attracts like". Let's look at this in terms of the thinking habits of unfocused people. Have you ever noticed in the workplace environment how a strongly negative person attracts other negative people and how they sap the energy and depress positive people? They tend to surround themselves with negative people that vibrate or harmonize with their negative core and vibes.

By the same token, positive people tend to surround themselves with other positive people. They energize and motivate others. The strongly negative person and strongly positive person don't mix well! A strongly negative person will drain all of the energy from a weaker positive person. A strongly positive person, on the other hand, will radiate, amplify, and charge up other weaker positive people.

If you are negative, depressed, angry, sick, and broke, you probably aren't very happy or doing very well. If you are still blaming your childhood, relatives, friends, parents, employer, government, or genetics (the list can go on and on here) for your current station in life, you are misguided. Your core is tainted and your thinking is twisted, but help and hope are right here, right now!

You can never move forward until you come to realization day and recognize the reason for your current station in life is facing you in the mirror! This is a hard internal battle for a lot of people still playing the blame game. Many negative people have spent their entire life negatively programming their subconscious core. They refuse to blame themselves and instead use the blame game as a logical, justifiable crutch that prevents them from ever achieving anything worthwhile in life. If they have a nice reasonable set of excuses for being a failure in life, they can remain a failure forever because they are not responsible for their life! They need to take control of their daily thoughts by reprogramming their subconscious core, thus their destiny!

These are not generally bad or evil people. They are just asleep and have not been awakened to the awesome power they possess! Just because someone has a negative core does not put them in the same hell as Hitler. Negative thoughts create and validate unworthiness, dependency, hopelessness, sickness, low self-esteem, low self-confidence, depression, low energy, no drive, purposelessness, aggression, hatred, and jealousy, etc. By replacing those negative thoughts with positive ones that make you feel more worthy, alive, and energized, you can generate real mind power! This is what I'm driving at here. You can change from negative to positive the moment you begin to control your thoughts! Liberation day can come your way, TODAY!

Liberation day is not the day to smash all of the mirrors in your house. It is a good day! Here's why: if the problem is "out there" and you blame outside forces and circumstances, then there isn't much you can do about that as an individual. However, if the problem is in your head, you can fix that right away. You can address that problem right NOW! You can fix that today! Aren't you glad you're reading this book?

WAKE UP!

CHAPTER 9

Reprogramming Your Subconscious Core—Taking Conscious Control of Your Frequency and Destiny, Today!—Tuning Your Mental Radio

There are two basic ways to reprogram your subconscious core. The first method is called "autogenic conditioning" and involves affirmations (self-talk) and/or visualization (imagineering). The second method involves working with a "deep trainer". The trainer works one-on-one with a person helping them to reprogram their subconscious core. I will explain these methods in enough detail so that you may practice them. However, an in-depth study of autogenic conditioning is found in my first book, *The Powermind System, Power of Will.*

Most people are constantly running negative self-talk programs in their conscious minds all day long. They think they "can't" do things, they "lack" something, or are "afraid" of something. They affirm these negative thoughts to themselves and out loud to others around them all day long!

They say things like: " I can't find a good job", "I can't seem to get promoted", "I lack training", "I lack education", "My job sucks", "I'm afraid to do that", " I can't afford it", "What if I get in trouble?", "I don't have enough money". All negative, all self-defeating, all self-sabotaging, all depressing—all bad core programming!

As a person affirms this incessant negativity and repeats it emotionally day after day, month after month, year after year, it all gets ingrained or programmed into their subconscious core. Through the law of attraction, these thoughts are then mirrored throughout their life in the experiences this person has and the life they lead. This thinking must be totally turned around!

The affirmed thoughts need to be positive to attract positive experiences, good health, people, money, events, ideas, etc. into your life. As I said in Chapter 1, the conscious mind can only hold one thought at a time. Through diligent "thought substitution" you can systematically replace all of the negative affirmations (thoughts) with positive ones.

Here's another example of how to practice this thought substitution method. Substitute something like this instead of the negative self-talk mentioned earlier: "I am the best at finding great jobs for myself" or "I am finding promotional opportunities often" or "I am well educated and continue to get smarter everyday" or "I am fearless and unstoppable". Substitute positive thoughts for the negative ones.

The sister technique is called visualization or imagineering. Most negative people are actually quite good at this! I call it negative goal setting, most people call it WORRYING! The negative person worries constantly. They visualize and emotionalize all of the horrible things that could happen to them, their families, and the world around them in vivid detail. This is an excellent way to turn your subconscious core completely negative!

While you are replacing negative worry images with positive visualizations, try to "see" in your mind's eye all of the wonderful things that "could" happen to you, your family, and the world around you. Imagine these things in vivid detail with high energy positive emotions.

Using a "deep trainer" is the second method I will discuss here. A "deep trainer" can assist you in creating and programming your affirmations and visualizations while you are in a clear, lucid, focused state. They help you along in the reprogramming process. You affirm out loud to them your visions, goals, mental images, and emotional responses to your personal deep desires. They aid in subconscious core rebuilding.

By following the techniques described above, you alter your subconscious core. You in turn alter the vibrational frequency of your superconscious mind by induction and tune in to a different mental radio station. You become in tune or tuned in to people, places, events, and ideas that will help you achieve what you are programming into your subconscious core. You switched the mental radio station from negative to a new positive one. Now, you can fine tune your awareness to focus on the exact things and information you need depending on the clarity of your goals.

By setting your goals with definite purpose, crystal clarity, disciplined focus, concentration, and tuning your mind, you will get exact results. This is how it works, this is the LAW!

"One draws to himself thought waves corresponding in character with the nature of the prevailing thoughts in his own mind-his mental attitude. Then again he begins to set in motion the great law of attraction, whereby he draws to him others likely to help him, and is in turn, attracted to others who can aid him."

William Walker Atkinson
Author of, *Subconscious and Superconscious Planes of Mind*

CHAPTER 10

Attracting Your Desires with Superconscious Thought Induction— Soul Power and Radiant Energy

Everyone realizes their body generates and radiates heat in the form of infrared radiation or heat waves. This is nothing new. You can see your heat signature with an infrared camera. The heat field obviously extends beyond your physical body. This is one form of a "radiant energy" field.

Your nervous system and brain operates using electricity generated from chemical reactions in your cells. This makes an electrical field around your body. All electricity also generates a magnetic field. So, you have a magnetic energy field as well. This is not shocking new science, this is a fact. I'm just talking about basic high school biology and physics here.

You radiate energy waves from your body on multiple frequencies all the time, none of which can be seen with the naked eye (by most people anyway). What controls the pattern of electrical impulses and magnetic field radiating from your body, brain, and mind? Your thoughts, of course! This is why I am focusing so heavily on controlling your thoughts and thought patterns, because these control your radiant energy field around your body and frequency.

Your superconscious mind also generates energy and radiates that energy field around and outside of your physical body. The energy field can travel long distances and is not bound by the currently known laws of Newtonian physics as we understand them today.

When I was in school I learned about vibration, frequency, amplitude, and subatomic particles. I then learned that much is totally unknown and some of what I learned was flat-out wrong! Even today's physicists don't know all of the physical laws governing vibration and energy. A new field of physics called quantum physics was formed where current Newtonian physical laws actually do NOT apply! This field was born out of new discoveries and the fact that Newtonian physics breaks down when you go subatomic or quantum!

Once we enter the realm of quantum physics, new physical laws apply and there are many yet to be discovered. Quantum physicists today are perplexed by the many anomalies they can't currently explain.

I do not claim to have all of the answers and details in regard to superconscious thought wave technology. I do however know precisely how it works in applying the principles successfully in a person's life. I do not know all of the circuitry involved in how a laptop computer works either, but I can operate one pretty well—and so can you!

We know we radiate energy from our bodies—this is fact. Our minds radiate superconscious thought energy, frequencies determined by your subconscious core thoughts. We know by the law of attraction we can influence and attract those like frequencies into our lives and create our realities. This is all fact!

These are the principles of superconscious thought induction. These principles show us how to consciously control our thoughts to positively manifest in our lives the environment, relationships, health, and wealth we desire, and they also explain our current station in life. The power of your mind goes well beyond what can easily be explained by known physical laws.

This is truly superhuman living compared to how most people think about themselves and their lives. When they are not "tuned in" to their superconscious power, they look at their immediate circumstances in life as a "helpless observer", not a "creator" of their life and destiny.

This can all begin to change for you immediately, once you become aware of who you are, what you are made of, what your connection is with the whole, and your willingness to look inside yourself for true answers. Your superconscious mind has tremendous soul power that most people are not aware of and certainly never tap into!

Napoleon Hill's Invisible Counselors

Napoleon Hill conducted one of the most extensive research projects on successful people in U.S. history. He spent more than twenty years personally interviewing successful men of his day to glean their success secrets. His landmark book, *Law of Success,* details his life's work. The title "Law of Success" is important! The core of this book was later published as, *Think and Grow Rich,* which has sold millions of copies worldwide. That title is important too!

As Hill conducted his interviews with people, he uncovered an interesting superconscious power that he personally experimented with. He called it his "invisible counselors". The technique initially terrified Hill even though he was well schooled in mind science at the time. He thought he was losing his mind and stopped after a few short weeks. Years later, he came back to it and was able to master the method to great advantage in building his self-confidence, personal fortune, career and unique problem solving abilities. He then continued to use the technique for the rest of his life. Hill had actually stumbled upon an advanced superconscious thought induction method.

The technique is as follows. Each evening before going to sleep, Hill would close his eyes and imagine a special meeting around a large conference table with him seated at the head. He would then summon his ten imaginary counselors to their assigned seats. He selected the men for specific reasons because he wanted to aquire certain mental aspects from each of them. Some of the men were living at the time, others were dead!

For example: he selected Thomas Edison to gain Edison's inventive genius. He selected Henry Ford to gain industrial production knowledge, Andrew Carnegie for wealth creation. Other men on his initial list included: Luther Burbank, Thomas Paine, Abraham Lincoln, and Napoleon.

He would go around the table and ask each of the men to give him the traits he desired from them. Later he would ask them to solve problems he was working on. At first not much happened. But as time went on, he felt they were giving him the traits he desired and helping him solve his problems with unique ideas. Then they became animated in his mental meetings and began to speak. Soon after that, they would no longer listen to Hill and began side conversations and got unruly with each other. This terrified Hill and he immediately stopped! Later in life, Hill learned greater mental discipline and started the meetings again and was able to control all of the men. He said he used the technique for the rest of his life to great personal advantage. He also would swap out and bring in new members as time passed.

Hill was using his superconscious power to not only communicate with the living on a subconscious level but also tap into universal thought patterns left behind by the men who had died. Later in life Hill recognized nearly the full scope of his mental capabilities.

"Anything I want or need or desire in life, I simply reach out my hand and close it. I am in perfect health and have acquired wealth and wisdom beyond my dreams."

Napoleon Hill
Author of, *Law of Success*

CHAPTER 11

Scientific Proof of Superconscious Power—Quantum Physics and the Tuning Fork Experiment

The concept of you radiating out energy from your superconscious mind of a specific frequency bundle, or specific frequency mix, is uniquely analogous to the tuning fork experiment. The tuning fork experiment goes like this: if you take two G note tuning forks mounted atop isolated wooden boxes and then hit one to start it vibrating, within a second the other one will start vibrating in harmony, although the second fork was never PHYSICALLY touched.

This is not totally shocking. What is shocking, however, is the fact that the G tuning fork cannot vibrate any other tuning fork placed next to it except another G fork. It is the same with all tuning forks. They can only vibrate, induce or amplify other tuning forks of the SAME frequency!

A G fork has no effect on an E fork, or any other fork. It only affects forks tuned to the G frequency. Moreover, if two G forks are already vibrating in harmony with each other, and you hit one really hard to amplify its vibration, the other G fork will ramp up its vibrations to match the first fork's vibration. The two will always vibrate in harmony, even though the second fork was never physically touched!

This is an important principle in regards to superconscious thought induction. After harmonic frequency is established between two people, the stronger of the two can always ramp up and amplify the other. Also, once you vibrate on a certain frequency you tune in to other people on the same frequency. Did you ever meet someone and you just seemed to click? That person is on the same core frequency as you are!

When I was in school, I learned the universe is composed of matter and energy, and that matter is composed of atoms. Atoms are composed of three subatomic particles called protons, neutrons, and electrons. That is it. Quantum physics has proven that this model is totally incorrect. There are many, many more subatomic particles. They are all constantly in motion, vibrating at ultra high speeds, generating and emitting energy fields.

The great physicist Niels Bohr discovered all "particles" (matter) have both a wave component and a particle component. It is referred to as the dual wave particle nature of matter.

Today, we learn from quantum physics that there is no matter at all! There are only packets of energy made of nothing but whirling waves of energy.

If you would like to see the look of shock and terror on the face of a quantum physicist, just ask them about the "measurement problem", which is related to the "Heisenberg uncertainty principal". This principal says that the exact position of an electron cannot be measured. The position actually depends on the OBSERVER!

But wait! There's more. The electrons don't just vibrate. They actually "pop" in and out of existence! Totally bizarre!

Current quantum physicists have many such problems in regard to the nature of matter and energy that are unresolved and unknown at this point in our existence. That is a fact!

The double slit electron experiment is classic in demonstrating this odd phenomenon. It shows how an electron can behave as both a particle or a wave, depending on the observer or on it being measured.

Well, what is my point by digressing into quantum physics here (where I probably lost many of you)? My point is this. As far as science can understand today, you are made up of a collection of atoms, and on a subatomic level the atoms are made up of pure energy! So, you are in reality a composite of pure energy guided by a will. This is a fact and it does not depend on your faith or belief system.

It is not relevant if you are a religious person, atheist, physicist, metaphysicist, scientist, witch or surgeon. The fact remains you are energy controlled by a conscious will and influenced by others and to a greater degree, a collective consciousness (which most people call God).

The "energy" and "conscious will" concepts are the two points that you need to grasp here for the purpose of this book. Don't worry about understanding all of the quantum physics. No quantum physicist understands all that either!

In our society today, there is a disconnect between science, religion, medicine and metaphysics. A day will arrive when they all come together. Every physicist, scientist, geneticist, religious researcher, etc. that searches comes to realize, in their quest for knowledge and truth, that there are things yet to be explained about the powers and forces at work in our lives and in our world.

Interesting quotes for your consideration:

"The supernatural is the natural not yet understood."
Elbert Hubbard
Author of, *The Message to Garcia*

"Everyone who is seriously involved in the pursuit of science becomes convinced that a Spirit is manifest in the Laws of the Universe."
Albert Einstein

"I believe that the mind has the power to affect groups of atoms and even tamper with the odds of atomic behavior and that even the course of the world is not predetermined by physical laws but may be altered by the uncaused volition of human beings."

Sir Arthur Stanley Eddington
English mathematician and astrophysicist

CHAPTER 12

Direct Effects of Superconscious Thought Induction—Attracting People, Events, Ideas, and Plans— Boosting Your Immune System, Too!

"What the fool cannot understand, he laughs at,
thinking by his laughter he shows superiority,
rather than latent idiocy."

Marie Corellie

There are multiple possible types of superconscious thought induction effects. The greater your clarity, focus, drive, and persistence, the greater the effects.

Attracting the right people is probably the most common superconscious effect. Through programming your subconscious core, you automatically begin to set in motion the superconscious process that will begin attracting people into your life for a specific reason. These people usually have important information or can offer tremendous aid in accomplishing your goal.

"Events" will also manifest themselves as a superconsious thought induction effect. All of a sudden you start to become aware of events that start to happen in your favor, speeding you to your goal. Most people wrongly attribute this to chance or luck. These are not lucky breaks at all! These events are not random. They happen because you preprogrammed your core and you asked for it! You may not know all of the details of how or why this event will help you. You will, however, get a strong sense of being in the right place at the right time. Your intuition will be your guide here and it will not fail you!

You can experiment with this and prove it to yourself in your own life by keeping a personal journal. Through tracking all of your "lucky breaks" by date, which are directly related to your preprogrammed goals, you will see there is no coincidence or luck involved at all. You will understand that the superconscious events are not random either.

Keep in mind superconscious thought induction is extremely powerful. Be sure to consciously control and attract what you want through positive thoughts.

Ideas and plans are yet another fascinating superconscious thought induction effect. The idea tends to be simple and unique while the plan tends to be exact and to work out perfectly. A blast of insight or flash of inspiration might lead you to exclaim "Ah-Ha...I've got it!"

Did you ever go to sleep stewing or focusing on a difficult problem you were facing? Then perhaps in a dream, in the middle of the night, or first thing in the morning you were "struck" with the perfect solution, idea, or plan? This can be a consciously controlled, refined and honed skill you can develop and apply successfully throughout your life.

There are numerous ways people have experienced miraculous healings as a result with superconscious thought induction. Western allopathic medicine focuses on treating the symptoms of a disease, using shots, pills, drugs, surgeries, and radiation to cure almost every ailment, from colds to cancer, these treatments all have their place in healing.

However, there are many things we are beginning to understand that have not found their way into mainstream health care yet—energy healing with superconscious thought induction being one of them!

Even most practiced physicians of Western allopathic medicine will admit a patient's attitude or mental state will greatly affect, either positively or negatively, the outcome of surgical recovery and a patient's general wellness. Your immune system responds immediately to positive or negative thoughts. Positive thoughts boost it tremendously!

CHAPTER 13

Becoming Superhuman—Developing Unstoppable Drive and Persistence—The Human Electromagnet Analogy

"You are searching for the magic KEY that will unlock the door to the source of power; and yet you have the KEY in your own hands, and you make use of it the moment you learn to control your thoughts."

Napoleon Hill
Author of: *Law of Success,*
Mental Dynamite,
Think and Grow Rich

As your awareness grows of your mental capablilities you will start to see superconscious thought induction in operation in your own life and in the lives of those around you. You will develop keen observation skills and a strong belief in what you have learned so far in this book.

I am always encouraging my students to keep a detailed personal journal with them at all times to write down superconscious effects, their dates, times of occurence, details, etc. Over time, if you continue with personal journaling, you will start to see specific superconscious patterns developing in your life. The type of effects, speed of occurence, impact of effects, correlation with your conscious state of mind, emotions, amplification, sickness, health, and well-being will be obvious. These will all begin to have striking connections that are visible on paper for you to evaluate and analyze. My booklet titled, "The Secret Power of Personal Journals" will help you out a lot here.

It is all of these types of factors that we are carefully researching, documenting and profiling with our students at The Powermind Institute for Advanced Psychic Research and Energy Healing. Here our students get a wealth of information from world-renowned authors, lecturers, scientists, and health care professionals of various backgrounds.

The students are then able to use this information to greatly enhance their lives and the lives of others. Our students and teachers come from all walks of life. The students come to us eager to learn more about themselves and the power of superconscious thought induction. Others come to be mentally and physically healed or explore their natural talents and genetic skills. They learn the principles of creating experiences for the enjoyment and benefit of all. Many times we will take the tough cases when families have nowhere else to turn to or no one else to call. We work with: terminal illness, post traumatic stress syndrome, depression, drug addiction, chronic pain, indigo children, suicide, unexplainable abilities, etc. Sometimes we are the tool of last resort, simply because we understand and see what others cannot. Many people have family members young and old that have gone down the standard track for mental or physical help and nothing has worked. We have staff and files and have searched, researched and seen a lot more than an ordinary person—things the average person never even suspected existed. Contact us, we are here to help!

As you become more aware of your superconscious power by tracking events, journaling, discovering patterns and enhancement techniques you will realize you have a much larger degree of control over that which you previously thought you had no control over at all.

Through your own personal life experiences, you will develop unshakeable, unwavering belief, drive, and persistence. You will "know" what you can be, have, and do by using "superhuman superconscious power" to make it happen!

CHAPTER 14

Mental Shielding—Building Impenetrable Psychic Armor

Most people are totally unaligned between their conscious, subconscious and superconscious minds and therefore mentally weak. As soon as they run into a small challenge, they quit. They let some little insignificant set-back stop them dead in their tracks. These people will not achieve anything meaningful in life.

Sometimes the challenges to alignment are much greater. Family members, close friends, a partner—or one of the worst I have seen, a "negative spouse"—all of these pose great challenges to mental alignment. These negative people know exactly which emotional buttons to push to get straight to your core, defuse your superconscious energy and prevent alignment.

As an example, a good friend of mine, whom I had known for many years, always had the dream and desire of starting his own business. He already had the knowledge, money, ability, etc. He did not, however, have his wife's support.

His wife constantly filled him with fear, degrading his self-confidence and self-esteem. They had a good relationship in many ways, but on this particular issue, she transferred her fears directly into him. She drilled fear and negativity into his subconscious core every time the topic came up.

My friend and I parted many years ago, on good terms, and I ran into him not long ago. I asked him how his job was going. He told me he doesn't get along with his boss and that when he goes to sleep at night he is terrified he will lose his job. I asked him how long that had been going on in his head, to which he replied, "YEARS!"

I asked him if he was still married to the same woman, he said, "Yes." I found this very interesting indeed! He could have started his own business years ago and left his fears behind. Instead he chokes on the dust of his own regret every single night!

As an individual you must totally be committed to your goals one hundred percent! You must not waiver. You must be aligned and in harmony with your conscious, subconscious, and superconscious minds. All bridges for retreat and escape must be burned!

This cannot be a haphazard wish or dream or whim in your head. You must place yourself on a disciplined mental training regime. This takes great courage and strength to face your past programming. It takes even more discipline to face the present head-on and monitor and shield your core from negative daily attacks.

Negative people must be eliminated from your personal atmosphere. If they cannot be totally eliminated, at least contact with them should be minimized, and proper attention given to all of the negative words you may hear from these people so you can counteract them immediately with thought substitution. You must shut those words out. Do not let those words enter your subconscious core.

Other negative people like co-workers, friends, neighbors, relatives must also be held to this rule! You must avoid core-damaging people as much as you can!

You must also eliminate negative television programming, radio, music, video games, and violence in general. The more you reduce your exposure to negativity, and consciously resist it impacting your subconscious core, the stronger and healthier you will become on all levels.

You must consistently immerse yourself in thinking about your goals, while surrounding yourself with a positive supporting network of people. People who will motivate you, energize, support, and build your core. These are the people you want in your inner circle.

By doing this you are building your impenetrable psychic shield of armor! Systematically weed out negative thoughts and thought patterns. Limit contact with negative people, places, music, and all distractions that affect you in a negative way. Consciously replace negative self-talk with a more positive outlook or vision for yourself and your future. It takes one positive thought, followed by another. You always have the present moment choice to make a conscious shift to a better positive way of thinking, believing and living! You can do this right now!

"The Magnetic Mask achieves effectiveness when it covers personal state and purpose in a manner positively to attract, and in that manner alone."

Dr. Frank Channing Haddock
Author of, *The Power Book Library*

CHAPTER 15

Amplifying Powers—Matching Alignment with Another, Entrainment, and Accelerating Superconscious Effects

Another superconscious feature to be aware of is that if two people are perfectly aligned spiritually, mentally, and physically (triple bonded) and focused on a common goal in each other's subconscious cores they can amplify their superconscious power exponentially. It is similar to the tuning fork experiments I discussed in an earlier chapter. This triple bond between two people however, is near impossible to accomplish.

It is difficult enough for one person to achieve perfect mental alignment by themselves but adding another person complicates the mental energy system dramatically. There are many disciplined requirements that must be met by both partners. The first of which is that a superconscious (spiritual) or soul connection must pre-exist. This type of connection cannot be trained, manufactured, or brought into existence by sheer power of will. A spiritual connection either exists or it does not.

Second, the two partners must maintain consistent daily contact and work hard to maintain perfect harmony with each other on all three levels—physical, mental, and spiritual. One partner must also be the dominant driver (leader) of the pair. This is either set at the start based on initial contact of the two or agreed upon at the outset in a pact between the two. The two partners will then enter into this pact bonded together to continuously balance, feed, enhance, and build off each other's energy. This is a full on superbonded pair! The ultimate in superconscious power!

Another type of partnership, although not quite as powerful, is a mental and spiritual connection between two people as they strive together towards a common goal. They team up, so to speak, for example, business partners. The superconscious effects are pronounced.

The third type of amplification, which is intensely interesting, is the use of "entrainment". In technical terms, this means mental frequency synchronization and amplification between two people. In less technical terms, it means the two become "in-tune" with each other on a subconscious core level. The dominant partner or "trainer" can control the amplification and raise the other person's core frequencies, strengthening, balancing, and healing them. This is what I refer to as a "deep trainer". This process may lead to pair bonding down the road. Use of a "deep trainer" requires discipline by the student and total commitment to the process. This is very different than the relationship between a "therapist" and "client" where you simply download your problems weekly and are then prescribed a daily dose of a mind-numbing drug.

Our Powermind Institute has "deep trainer" faculty, but they only accept a limited number of people to work with, help and heal.

CHAPTER 16

Three Real-Life Examples of Superconscious Power— Prisoner to Preacher, Jet Setting Around the World and Saving a Life That had a Purpose!

Prisoner to Preacher

My first book, *The Powermind System, Power of Will,* sells internationally and oddly enough has gained widespread acceptance in the U.S. corrections system as a rehabilitation guide, although that was not my intended target audience. I am not complaining though—whoever gains relief, good health, wisdom, and turns from negative to positive influence by my works, more power to them!

This particular offender was from the maximum security prison in Oak Park Heights, Minnesota. I have spoken there before to both staff and population. The offender wrote me a letter in 2000 describing his plight in life and recounting his life story to me. He said he was raised in the government housing projects (referred to as "Crack Stacks") in downtown Minneapolis. All he knew while growing up was drugs, gangs, dealers, and violence. At the age of 17, he was tried as an adult and convicted of a felony and sentenced to prison for 10 years. After that, he was in and out of prison for the next 30 years! His brother was in the same situation, both repeat offenders and hard core criminals.

He happened upon my Powermind System book in the prison library and read it many times cover to cover. It affected his mind deeply. He had his brother study my book as well.

He was struck by the fact that his core was so totally negative and that he actually did have a good natural talent that he never capitalized on. When he was 6 or 7, he said he used to watch television preachers and then would stand on the coffee table at his apartment and "preach" what he heard on television. Neighbors, adults, and kids alike would come over to watch him "preaching" on the table and were amazed. My Powermind book, seminars, and talent tests show people how to determine their natural talents and genetic skills with great accuracy. He realized he actually had a natural talent through one of my book tests.

Two years later in 2002, he finished serving his last sentence, was set free, enrolled in seminary school, became an ordained minister, founded his own church, recruited his brother to help with his church, and now preaches to ex-offenders at his church to help them turn their lives around! All that is not just dumb luck! He aligned his mind on a specific positive goal.

Jet Setting Around the World

V is a woman I worked with for many years. I spotted her natural talents in one of my leadership seminars. I found out quickly she was unhappy with her 9–5 day job. She felt totally stifled and that she could do so much more. However, she was mentally stuck and initially lacked the self-confidence to start her own event planning business—an industry she worked in. I told her to go for it! I told her she had it in her to achieve her dream. She was hesitant. She faced the same types of fears most people face when seriously considering starting their own business.

Over a period of months (and now years) I worked with her as my student and trained her not only in the Powermind System, but in superconscious power as well. She had the goal of starting and running her own business and jet setting around the world for a long time. In less than 6 months from the time she made the total mental core commitment to do it, she actually started her business and quit her day job. She obtained a huge contract right off the bat. Exactly what she needed, perfectly timed!

V has now organized, concept to completion, dozens of events in exotic destinations all over the world for high end business clients. She has visited Stonehenge and felt the rocks, kissed the Blarney Stone. She has flown on private business jets and makes a great income that she would have never ever made in her previous job. She has complete confidence, acute business savvy and excellent negotiation skills. She has more time off to spend as she chooses with her family—more than she would have ever had in her 9–5 job. She now controls her own business, her own income and…her life! She also has true understanding of what she is capable of. She brought her dream into reality. More recently she was offered an awesome full-time day job in her industry by a large firm and simply declined the offer! I was able to help enhance her core and awaken her spirit and there is no turning back after that! Her mind and life were evolutionized!

Saving a Life That had a Purpose

Saving a life that had a purpose is my third example, although I have dozens more! I recall a young boy about 8 years old who did not know how to swim. He was playing in a river with his older sister and some of her friends. Suddenly he lost his footing and the current swept him a hundred yards or so downstream to a narrow concrete dam opening where the water was very deep and rapid. The boy recalled seeing the sky intermittently as he was underwater in the current. He kept going under gasping for air and screaming for help! He recalls going through the deadly concrete opening of the dam, reaching out with his left hand. Finally, his hand found the concrete. He was able to climb up on it, his hands and feet bleeding from scraping on the rocks in the river. He stood up and walked across the dam wall to shore. A few minutes later his sister, her friends and mother arrived thinking he was dead somewhere downstream. Shocked to see him standing, they were all grateful. The little boy, of course, was me! This was my first near-death experience. Just a "lucky break" right? Others much older and stronger died in that river. Why not me? Superconscious power can be induced immediately in critical life-saving circumstances! A number of books have been written about superconscious thought induction in life threatening situations—it is called the "third man phenomenon".

CHAPTER 17

Are You a Scanner?
Relatively Few Are.

In 1972, the CIA funded a top secret MJ12 (Majestic 12) research project code named "Project Scanate". The project was inspired by rumors that the Russians were using psychics in military operations. The top secret U.S. project focused on the investigation of paranormal abilities in certain "gifted" people and the potential for using people with such abilities in intelligence-gathering operations. This was the first time in history the CIA would fund true research into psychic abilities. In the 1970s, Dr. Harold Puthoff and Russell Targ of the Stanford Research Institute (SRI) partnered with the CIA to investigate people with psychic abilities.

They were initially interested in many areas of psychic abilities, but focused on astral projections (out-of-body experiences) or superconscious travel and using mentally "matched pair" partners.

The project evolved over the years into other projects, called "Grill Flame" and "Gondola Wish", all of which were funded by military units until the early 1990s when it was finally called "Project Stargate" and was ended (Questionable?).

At Princeton University, the Princeton Engineering Anomalies Research (PEAR) lab started by Dr. Robert G. Jahn, Professor Emeritus of Aerospace sciences worked with ESP. His groundbreaking scientific research into psychic abilities with his research partner Brenda J. Dunne resulted in their landmark book "Margins of Reality" where they describe controlled scientific psychic research experiments and results.

Some people are highly psychically gifted "scanners", others can be trained, amplified, and enhanced. There are also some popular names for specially gifted children as well, which are "indigo children", "crystal children", and "new children". There are many categories of psychic abilities and a few have yet to be discovered. I describe these abilities in my new book "Are You a Psychic Scanner". My term scanner is a spin-off term from Project Scanate, simply referring to people with advanced natural talents in many areas of psychic or superconscious power. My research for the Powermind Project has a special branch The Powermind Institute for Advanced Psychic Research and Energy Healing that now studies the scanner phenomenon in both children and adults. I have several specially-trained faculty at my institute who dedicate time and effort into this research to find scanners, study them, profile their abilities, and train them. We are also tracing genetic inheritance of abilities and DNA mutations. We are especially interested in identifying abilities early in children and teenagers in order to track genetic inheritance and genes in family trees.

If you:

- felt like there was something different about you since you were a child,
- have difficulties connecting and fitting in with groups of people,
- have ever had an out-of-body experience,
- get strong intuition about people on first meeting them,
- vividly remember your dreams,
- can persuade and influence large groups of people with ease,
- have had a miraculous healing or near death experience,
- can predict future events,
- have regular "déjà vu" experiences,
- can't relate on a deep level to your partner,

then you might be a scanner!

We have specialized tests, personality profiles, training courses, counseling and well schooled faculty available and we are interested in you.

Help is right here, right now!
www.powermindtraining.com

"I believe that the science of chemistry alone almost proves the existence of an intelligent Creator."

Thomas A. Edison
Electrical Scientist and Inventor

CHAPTER 18

The Powermind Institute for Advanced Psychical Research and Energetic Healing

We have a wide variety of unique products and specialized services, and seminars available! We are also interested in all research partnerships with other organizations, medical facilities, hospitals, hospices, correctional facilities, rehabilitation centers, universities, schools, churches, sports coaches/teams, military and government agencies.

Powermind System
Products • Keynotes • Seminars • Retreats • Testing • Personal Training

Products:

- *The Powermind System, Power of Will* (Book)
- The Powermind Natural Talent and Genetic Skills Test
- The Powermind Personality Profiling Test
- The Secret Power of Personal Journals (Booklet)
- Practical Mental Influences and Mental Fascination (Booklet)
- Millionaire Mindset — Secret Strategies of Self-Made Millionaires (Booklet)
- Control Your Destiny (Booklet)
- Super Speed Reading — How to Double Your Reading Speed in One Hour Flat (Booklet)

Order online at: **www.powermindtraining.com**

Keynotes:

Michael accepts a limited number of keynote engagements per year on a variety of topics, from achievement to life skills, to superconscious power, scanners, genetic inheritance, natural talents and energy healing.

Seminars:

Michael specializes in seminars and workshops designed to train people in personal performance techniques. His business seminar series includes: time management, project management, personality styles, high performance team building, talent management, sales, customer service, memory skills, speed reading, self-motivation, inspiration, goal setting, etc.

His other division under the Powermind Institute includes: gaining clarity of purpose, mental alignment, clearing chatter, superconscious thought induction, stress reduction, overcoming depression, healing chronic and terminal illness, raising gifted indigo children, the power of persistence, amplifying abilities with others, subconscious core rebuilding, childhood regression therapy, general wellness, post traumatic stress syndrome, rehabilitation, addiction, suicide, marriage counseling, etc.

Go to: **www.powermindtraining.com**

Connect with Michael Monroe Kiefer Ph.D. on **Linked in**.

Retreats:
Two and three day specialty retreat programs for corporate, family or personal training can be delivered to small or large groups around the world.

Contact our international event planner at: www.KeystoneEC.com

Life Coaching:

Michael and his unique research team accept a limited number of students per year for: career coaching, relationship building, personal finances, personal growth, life purpose, natural talents, counseling, mental enhancement training, childhood regression therapy, subconscious core rebuilding, superconscious thought induction, energy healing, etc.

Children • Teen • Family • Marriage:

- Dealing with difficulties in any of these areas or simply want to improve?
- Also how to raise "unique" children.
- Guidance on raising "gifted", "indigo" kids.

Testing and Diagnosis:

Diagnosing children and adolescents for genetic inheritance of "abilities", adult mental testing, raising and understanding "unique", " indigo" children and teens, encouraging and enhancing mental abilities, defining talent areas, superconscious thought induction, energy healing.

Visit us at:

www.powermindtraining.com

Connect with Michael Monroe Kiefer Ph.D. on **Linked** in.

CHAPTER 19

About the Author—Inception of The Powermind Institute for Advanced Psychical Research and Energetic Healing

B orn June 3, 1963 in Albany, New York, Michael experienced two near-death experiences and many astral projections before the age of 12. His remarkable academic achievements were expressed early in elementary school, where he bypassed most other students, especially in reading and writing. Michael accelerated his education and graduated from high school with honors in just three years. In high school, Michael was awarded the Teachers Association Scholarship for outstanding academic achievement.

Michael started college at the age of 17 at the State University of New York at Buffalo, majoring in cell and molecular biology and minoring in abnormal psychology. He was on the Dean's list almost every semester and was inducted into two National Latin Honor Societies for outstanding academic achievement.

Michael graduated in 1984 with his Bachelor of Science degree (cum laude). He then enrolled at Texas A&M University and graduated with a Master of Science degree and ABD in genetic engineering in 1988. His studies in world religions and paranormal activities continued throughout his college career. Michael holds a Ph.D. (magna cum laude) from Addison University in psychology and his dissertation research was on conscious, subconscious and superconscious interaction.

Michael ran a multi-million dollar DNA fingerprinting research lab for 7 years after graduating. During this time he founded the Powermind research project on human potential. His research team studied peak performers for over 12 years, searching for their genetic and psychological traits in family lineages. His stunning research results in this field were published in 1996 in *The Powermind System, Power of Will* book which is sold internationally and is the modern day hand book for personal power and mind science.

Since that time, Michael has traveled nationally doing keynotes, workshops, coaching and retreats for organizations as well as mental discipline training for a limited number of "specially gifted" students. In 2000, Michael assembled a specialized team of unique mentalists along with his elite students and continued intensive studies on the scanner phenomenon and the Powermind Institute was born. Michael has had other near-death experiences and miraculous healings since 2000.

Michael is a nationally recognized expert in the field of mind science and scanners. He continues to research, lecture, counsel, and train. He has developed numerous psychological profiling tests in the areas of natural talent and genetic skills, personality profiles, psychic abilities, human performance enhancement, motivation, and success. Michael and his personal team are focused on continued research in energy healing, the scanner phenomenon, "indigo" children, third man phenomenon, genetically inherited traits, quantum physics, subconscious core rebuilding, superconscious thought induction, and enhanced amplified pairs training. Michael is interested in creating public awareness, business partnerships, medical grant and research partnerships, as well as corporate performance training programs.

Help is right here, right now!
www.powermindtraining.com

Connect with Michael Monroe Kiefer Ph.D. on **Linked in**.

"Use the Magic Key with intelligence, and only for the attainment of worthy ends, and it will bring you enduring success. Forget the mistakes you have made and the failures you have experienced. Quit living in the past, for do you not know yesterdays never return? Start all over again, if your previous efforts have not turned out well, and make the next five or ten years tell a story of success that will satisfy your most lofty ambitions.

Make a name for yourself and render the world a great service, through ambition, desire and concentrated effort! You can do it if you BELIEVE you can!

Thus endeth the Magic Key."

Napoleon Hill
Author of, *Outwitting the Devil*

EPILOGUE

An Intelligent Man

"They (Saul, Barnabas, John) traveled through the whole island until they came to Paphos. There they met a Jewish sorcerer named Bar-Jesus, who was an attendant of the proconsul, Sergius Paulus. The proconsul, an intelligent man, sent for Barnabas and Saul because he wanted to hear the word of God. But Elymas the sorcerer (for that is what his name means) opposed them and tried to turn the proconsul from the faith. Then Saul, who was also called Paul, filled with the Holy Spirit, looked straight at Elymas and said, "You are a child of the devil and an enemy of everything that is right. You are full of all kinds of deceit and trickery. Will you never stop perverting the right ways of the Lord? Now the hand of the Lord is against you. You are going to be blind, and for a time you will be unable to see the light of the sun."

Immediately mist and darkness came over him, and he groped about, seeking someone to lead him by the hand. When the proconsul saw what had happened, he believed, for he was amazed at the teaching about the Lord."

Acts 13, 6–12 NIV

Michael Monroe Kiefer Ph.D.